P9-BHY-107

A Quiet Place

**Coming from deep within
Connecting with our Father
and with friends.**

Ewart F. Brown

Edited by:
 Linda G. M. Brown

© Copyright 1999 by, Ewart F. Brown

Published by Action Publications,
Keizer, OR

Printed in the United States of America

ISBN Number: 1-891879-06-5

Dedication

With all my heart I dedicate this
Quiet Place
to Lynn, my wife,
who is often weaved into its texture
and who is the significant reason
for who I am today.

ACKNOWLEDGMENTS

The thought had passed my mind by miles that some day I should write a book. But that thought never came back. Maybe, not a book, but a compilation of my sermons in a book form. This was a closer possibility, but not an urgent one.

Today, in your hand, serenading your eyes, are treasures from my heart to your heart, born from my late night journeys and other life moments. What then brought these treasures, *A Quiet Place*, to these pages? While serving as the Pastor of the Lents Church in Portland, Oregon, it often became natural to include in my sermons, my thoughts in the color of poetry. These I prefer to refer to as "Inspirational Thoughts". A few members liked them. But one member, Fordie, seemingly liked them more, and always wanted copies. My wife, Linda, liked some of them, she had to, and I liked them most of all.

The pleasant pusher, was Nina. Her best friend, Cam and I played cricket together. And Nina often came to the games. Nina learned of my dream to ink my thoughts on paper. So whenever she met me at Church, on the phone, at a party or on the cricket field, she asked about my book of Inspirational Thoughts. She once added; "I will not stop bugging you until it is done." Thanks Nina. It is done.

One day I was sharing my "Dream" to Bill. And to me he said; "Ewart, do your dream. One should never dream unless one intends to do the dream." I have done my dream.

So my special thanks race to the Divine Agencies, the source of inspiration, to my wife Lynn, to Fordie and to Nina, the pleasant pusher, to Bill for his encouragement and support. Also, special thanks to several individuals and events, because it was while my mind wandered to these people and events, that these thoughts were born. And to you reader, thanks for connecting your heart to our Father's and to mine at this very moment, through
A Quiet Place.

Ewart F. Brown

TABLE OF CONTENTS

The enchanted moment
is born
when the rose bush
unfolds its pearl -
A Rose.
And there is laughter
and love.

Then that Rose reclines
into silence
for a little while
that someday it will
sing again
for you
for them
even sweeter.
And the
enchanted moment
is born again.

There is never a
sunrise
without a sunset

There is never a
starry sky
without a darkness

There is never a
party
without an occasion

There is never a
dream
without a sleep

There is never a
harvest
without a sowing

There is never a
finish line
without a starting

There is never a
future
without a present

Life has two faces

Thanks to God.

GOD IN THE DISTANCE

Even though God seems away
    in the distance
I know I must reach for Him
  for He is reaching for me
  and somehow, someday,
    I will see His face.

Even though God seems away
    in the distance
and His voice is faint or never heard
I feel the gentle breeze of His presence
    and I know He is close to me.

Even though God seems away
    in the distance
there is no time nor space between us
  for God is too big and too much,
      favoring me
  to plant Himself away from me.

Even though God seems away
    in the distance
His heart is touching mine
His hands are holding mine
And His tears are touching my tears.

Even though God seems away
   in the distance
         My trust is firm
         My heart is still
         For God is mine
         Forever mine.

So I talk to God
I walk with God
I rest in God
And nothing can
      come between
         God and me.

*I stretch my hand to You
You stretch Your heart to me*

LONELY

I left home this morning.
My destination, Church.
There are things at home
    waiting for me
But as at other times,
    they have no real warmth.
I surely hope that someone
        a Church person, at the Church
            will offer me that missing warmth.
And I will be filled and satisfied.

Surely, God, Jesus
 and the Holy Spirit are there.
They promised they would.
And faithful, they will.
But who else will be there?
Will there be hands, hearts and eyes
    like mine, to connect with?
Will there be even just one
    to understand my journey
        and to reach out to me?
I hope so.

Sometimes, the parking lot is a scary place
    and a safe place.

I feel safe to anchor there.
A scary place – because beyond,
   is the unknown.
A safe place – because here I am and
    no one to hurt me.
Then comes the welcome lobby,
    filled with human voices.
And here I come longing for, most of all,
    just one heart
      which beats like mine
        to still the wind of my past week.

To sit in a pew is a giant step, though,
  for some, it is an easy choice.
By whom may I sit
  and will be welcomed?
Will a familiar face choose to sit
  close to me
   to make me feel warm
     and at home?
Will I feel like a desolate island
  surrounded by clusters of verdant
      civilizations?
While the service is filled with smiles
   and singing
 only my heart understands
   what I am feeling for, longing for – like
    a personal, warm connecting heart
     that beats like mine.

This is the end of Church.
I wished it had never come.
Why does Church not go on and on?
For the end of Church, means to me;
    Lonely again
        A lonely car
        A lonely home
        A lonely lunch
        A lonely life
        A lonely week.
Oh, I wish the phone will ring
    on Tuesday, or Wednesday,
        or any day will do.
Only let the voice be warm and friendly.

You may wonder who I am.
And why did I with-hold my name?
Yes, you know me.
You know my name.
I attend your Church –
    sit in your pew
    shake your hand
    say goodbye
And you reply –
    "So long Lonely"

> ### *The best way to settle the dust*
> ### *Is not to step in it.*

SILENCE

When the moment of God's silence
   seems to thunder through the air
     then it is time to be still and wait.
For as light follows darkness,
   so God's voice follows His silence.

Silence annoys and frustrates our
    cluttered chambers.
For here, there are always activities.
But the missing ingredient is painfully
    in the distance
And that is, the treat of listening for God
     to speak.

Sometimes, in silence, God is loudly
     speaking.
He may not be in the thunder nor the roar.
But poised in the gentle stillness
    is our God, speaking
     in His loudest tone.

No wonder He said; "Be still."

The shopping list never includes the line;
    "God's silence"
For merchants never stock it
 since customers never buy it.

Yet God's storehouse clearly displays it
    as an item that brings
        color, character and credence to life
        and a musical expectancy
            as we wait for God to speak.
In fact, God's silence, is that free item
    freely given, only for asking.

Well Lord, help me not to urge You
    to come to me,
        until Your time matures.
Please teach me to wait in silence
        during Your silence.
And when, through Your silence
    Your delights for me are fulfilled
        then break through that silence
        and flood me with Your
            gentle wise, musical voice.
Then I will understand that God's silence
    is not - God is sleeping,
        but a plan in place
        just for me.

The power of the Lord is limited
by the will of mankind

LOVE

Love God
with the little you have.
Love God
with the much you have.
He is certain to love you
with all that He has.

His love like a velvet lace

encircles you
and touches
every breath you take.

This love was born
just for you.
So rest
So live, and
Love.

TROUBLED LITTLE TEAR-DROP

Somewhere
    hidden in the closet of the night
            is a cluster of care.
It is the agent of our heavenly Father
    He who was before the fallen tear-drops
And He who sobs at the fall of each
        tear-drop.

Little Tear-Drops
    when you fall
        you do fall into safety and welcome.

You are cared for even
        before you fall.
And even in the darkness
        there are hands and eyes
            to find you.
You will never be alone,
    nor be forsaken, you
        dear troubled little
            tear-drops.

Somewhere
    hidden in the closet of the night
            is a tear-drop.
It has fallen to the carpet of leaves.
It is so silent and secret.

It fears that someone, somewhere,
  might hear and not understand.

So troubled little tear-drop
    spends the night alone.

Somewhere
      fallen leaves do understand
        and they will cradle even little
              troubled tear-drops.
For fallen leaves embrace the air
    and make it into a bed
        for the troubled tear-drops.

Fallen leaves catch the darkness
      from the night
          and use it to protect
              little troubled tear-drops.
So why should troubled little tear-drops
    feel so alone?

Maybe, it is not the aloneness that itches.
Maybe, it is simply the pains.
For sometimes pains hurt,
    even though there is an embrace
        and care
          so near.
Little tear-drops wish
    someone, somewhere
      would sail the pains away
        to a distant valley
          beyond the hills

where they die for ever
and ever.
And little tear-drops
would never fall again.

Somewhere
someone loves troubled little
tear-drops.
He made the tear-drops.
He falls along, when they fall.
He collects them one by one
and dusts and shines them
to be placed beside His heart.

So Troubled Little Tear-drop,
the next time you are falling
look! God has a golden cup.
He is collecting treasures –
your troubled little tear-drops,
to cradle them beside His
sweet companionship.

Troubled Little Tear-drop
You are loved.

FINDING GOD

I had not seen God

until, in quietness I looked inside
and above my reach.
Then I knew that seeing Him
was as easy as a smile
if only one took time to be still
and looked for Him.

God, in his majesty is dressed in humor.
For He tickles the musical mind
of His child.
Sometimes He hides behind the darkness.
He wants to see who would come
searching for Him.

When God is found
there is light and laughter.
The stars and skies become brighter still.
The human heart becomes
a dancing garden.
And God's home becomes
the treasure of our soul.

Dear God and Father,
   let me search and find you.
For the quiet, verdant pasture
   which my soul seeks,
      rests in your hands.
So I stretch and I reach for you
      until I find you
         and touch You.

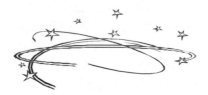

HEALTH FOR TODAY

Set your mind to the Sun Rise

Reach your hand up to the Skies

Ground your feet on the Rock

Place your heart in the Pleasant Past

And begin to enjoy Health

I LOVE YOU LORD

I have come Lord
    just to tell You that I love You.
I know that You will not wonder why.
But just in case You do, this is the reason;

      It is because You love me.
      You are wonderful to me.
      You are lovely.
      You are kind.
      You are just marvelous.
      You are everything.
      And as the river continues to flow,
       So does my heart,
       in praises to you.

Today is colored with sunlight
    and spotted with a few drops of rain.
Your gentleness and understanding
    are perched at my side.
And the only place to fall, is,
    in the ocean of Your loveliness
        and loving tenderness.

O Lord, please keep me here,
    close to You,
        forever.
And I will forever be loving You.

I love You Lord.

AT PEACE WITH GOD

When God awakens me in the morning,
 He lingers by my bedside,
  until I am fully composed
   and have set my course for the day.

As I sit in my corner
 to seek connection with Him, for the day
  He comes even closer to me
   to teach me His will
   to cord me to His heart, and
   to cover me with His power.

And when it is time to embark on
  the task for the day
 He moves into the chair next to me
   to be my mentor and my peace, and
   we work together
   we process together
   we take breaks and
   lunch times together
    and enjoy every moment.

Each day comes with a variety pack.
I experience smooth sailing days, and
I experience rough sea days.
But every day comes to me
 with God's warm assuring presence.

It's just amazing.
He promised that He would.
And surely, He has always been true.

What about the times
    when God seemed late
        and I had to go alone?
Or He had other chores
    and the call was mine alone?
Then I relied upon the times
    alone with Him,
        for His teachings are for every day
            and every occasion.

And when I acted just as He would
    the end results became
        His and my delight.
And I knew that truly,
    He was with me all along,
        even though I might have
            thought otherwise.
How could God stay away from me?
How could He leave a heart
    that is connected to His?
As the sun never loses sight of the earth,
    so my loving Father and God
        never loses sight of me.

O friend—
It is so amazingly warm,
    so comforting to walk with my God.

It is so reassuring to face the day,
   knowing, He is the day.

It is so peaceful to recline into His will,
   for His will is safe and sure.
It is immeasurably, amazingly lovely
   to be lost in God, where,
     I will never find a way out.
      And never desire to.

It is here where I find my peace.

GOD IS PULLING THE STRING
TO GET OUR ATTENTION

A FAVORITE PLACE

This is my favorite place
   the place of my desire,
      my supply and my filling.
This place surprises me, always
   because it returns to me
     more than I ever dreamed of
      or asked for.

I love this place, my favorite place
   the place of my peace,
     my quietness and reflection.
This place refreshes me
   because it lifts me and
     refocuses me
    to the eternal realities.
And I surely do need these.

I do look forward to my favorite place
   the place of companionship
   the place where my loneliness
     is exchanged for friendship,
      my desperation for fulfillment,
      my heart for His heart

And when I am there,
    I never want to leave.

Come, come to my favorite place
    the place where God meets me.
Here I put my bundles down
    fold myself into His arms
    feel His heart beat on my face
    and His fingers drying my
        dripping tears.

Come, come to my favorite place
    the place where God meets
      all those desiring a meeting place.
This place is close.
It's just a second away, a blink away.
It's easy to find.
Just look,
It's all around you.

Come, come to my favorite place.
Make it our favorite place,
    the place where God meets us
      and loves to meet us.
God cannot wait to meet us
    for he has sumptuous goodies for us.
And if you do not show up
    you may lose your share
      and hurt His heart.

Our favorite place
   is God's favorite place.
Here, God receives His affirmation,
      love and companionship.
So come.

Come often
   to our favorite place.
God is there
      stroking the leaves
        talking to the birds
          dancing in the shrubbery
            while waiting for us
              to show up.

Please, come to our favorite place,
   the meeting with God
      the gentle, kind God.
Just come, to this
   Favorite place.

There has never been a sunrise
Where there was never a darkness

JUST FOR TODAY

Lord,
Help me today, to
    Love you
      Love you
        And love you more

Lead me today, to
      Remember you
       Talk to you
        Talk about you
          And come back to you

O Lord, on this day
    Teach me, to
      Smile
       Sing
        Rest
         Walk
         Trust

Encourage me, to
    Offer a comforting thought
     Paint an amazing picture
      Leave behind an awesome wonder

And, to
    Pen a love letter
     Touch a child, a plant, a pet
      Build a bridge, a shelter, a roof
      Plant a garden with flowers

And whatsoever I may have missed
    please bring to my list
     that my love and service to you
      and others
       may be complete.

Ask not what plan God has for you today
Just ask that you be His plan.

WHAT HAPPENED TO YOUR HANDS

They were wounded for you.

One day he threw a spear at you.
It was rushing for your heart.
And I used my hands to protect you.
And the spear did a job on me.
That spear disfigured my hands.

Another day,
I met you struggling down a steep hill.
Your back was pasted with burdens too
    hard to carry.
Your feet bled from the glass like
    stone terrain.

And your tearful eyes spoke to me.
So I turned around and carried you.
It was then I slipped, and the stones
    tore my hands.

Do you remember the day
    I heard you crying?
That was the day your tree was too
    cumbersome and heavy.

You asked for help,
   but no one seemed to care,
      or even tried.
Then I came along.
You thought I was your only chance.

And so without delay, I took your tree,
   made it mine, to carry.
Well, that tree bruised my hands.

These hands, bruised and battered
   were the hands which saved your life.
For beneath the heavy load,
   laid your pressed, broken frame.
Your load had fallen on your chest and,
   no one cared, it seemed.
No one offered to help.
So I hurried to your side
   and lifted your load.

You see friend, in lifting this heavy load
      My hands were damaged.
So they bled and pained.
But it is alright
   since I did these for you
      because I love you.

This is what happened to my hands.

TALKING TO GOD

Once the heart has made
   contact with God
A spring of joy begins its journey
And life begins to bloom afresh
And there are flowers everywhere.

If the running brook could stop
   and Talk to God
It maybe, never would reach the beach.
If the humming bird knew
   where to find God
It maybe would sing in His presence and
   never leave again.

But you and I know the place of God.
We know the hour of God.
And there is no wind
   to wrench us from Him
For we are sunken, deeply, in God.

My heart no longer, longs for God
   like a plant reaches for the sun

For my voice calls Him to my side
And without a pause, He comes.

So I Talk to God
For He is just a whisper away
And my joys are sustained
And I cannot leave Him, ever again.
Friend, it matters not, day or night
The condition of my world
For my world is, God's heart.
It beats for me. It lives for me.
And all is well.

We don't have to be perfect Christians
We just need to be Christians who can
    Talk To God.
We don't have to be experts
We just need to be able to
    Talk To God.

We don't have to be on our knees
We just have to, from our hearts,
    Talk To God.
We don't have to turn our lips
We just have to turn our hearts and
    Talk To God.

We don't have to have needs and hurts
We may just want to praise, thank or,
	just Talk To God.
We don't have to Talk To God
We don't have to touch His heart.

But the more we Talk To God
The more answers He gives
And the more we desire
To Talk and Talk
	and
	Talk to God.

Prayer is the fingers we use
to hold God
close to our hearts.

FAR AWAY HOME

Far away
 far, far away
  around the distant bend
   is home, my home.

It seems so far.
It takes so long,
 that even a tree would stop,
  clasp its hands and
   wait for another day.

But the longer I wait
 the closer I am
  to home, my home.
And there,
 directions are meaningless
  for travel is by escort.
There, companionship is resplendent
 rest is lasting,
  sound and sweet.
For I have reached home,
 my home at last,
  Heaven.

THE DIFFERENCE

Life is a heartache
Life is a headache
Life is a bellyache
Life is an ache
     in this present state.
And what difference does it make?

Life is an invitation for –
     Stopping
     Sitting
     Looking to Jesus
     Trusting in Jesus
      in this present state.
And what difference does it make?

Life is a journey
Life is hope
Life is a partnership
Life is a delight
All because of Jesus
And what difference does it make?

A Prayer For Today

Lord, please make me your voice
      that speaks your heart
         to your people.

Touch my ears with yours
    that they may hear
    only as you hear.

Bind my eyes
  to see you
   and your creation.
Then I will be beautiful,
     inside.

Walk in front of me.
Guide me with your shadow
  and I will never be lost,
      again.

But most of all, Lord,
   please wrap me tightly
     in your sweet love.
Then I will know,
   that everything will be alright,
     for today and
      tomorrow.

TO GOD'S HEART

Call me Lord
  Let me know you still love me
Call me Lord
  Let me know how you care
Hold me Lord
  Let me never be alone again
Hold me Lord
  Till I am home again

Touch me Lord
  Let me feel your tender warmth
Walk me Lord
  Let me know we are friends
Teach me Lord
  Let me know your wisdom
Lead me Lord
  Let my foot steps be right

Hear me Lord
  Let me speak my troubles

Feed me Lord
   Let my feet be strong
Bless me Lord
   Let my life bear fruits for you
Save me Lord
   Let me know all is well.

Lord, this is my heart
   to your heart.

> **You might be a pin head
> in the universe
> But you are like a mountain
> In God's heart**

He Knew Me

He knew me
  so very well
So He drew me to Him.
And He gave me a place to sit
  close to Him.

He knew me
  so very well.
So He called me to come to Him.
For never would I have come,
  had He not called for me
    and pleaded with love.

He knew me
  so very well.
He knew that someday,
  I would ride high above
    the clouds,
      look into His face,
       and from His face,
  I would look to the faces painted
  with distress and tears.

O Lord, my God
  I am so glad you knew me
    and walked the path to find me.
My secrets are open for your pleasure.
So are my hands, my feet and lips.
But most of all,
  my heart.
O Lord, please never recline, until
    your heavenly will has imprisoned me,
      all of me.

*God has given you
a piece of His heart
When He gave you life*

CLIMBING TO
THE MOUNTAIN TOP

I began to climb the mountain.
Long, long, seemed
   the distance from base.
But in order to reach the top
  I had to climb,
    though long and trying the climb.

The scenery was rugged at times,
   with little pebbles of peace
      here and there.
The mountain lions roared.
The sparrows sipped
  from the dripping rocks.
And the winds danced from tree to tree.
There was even a smile from the sun,
     as if to say,
  "I remember you are there"

When I paused to rest a while,
  my mind drifted to the mountain top,
   but my feet remained
    in the gloom of reality –
    "I am not yet there"
And then I wondered,
  "Where am I going
  Why am I going

Will I ever get there and when?"
Then suddenly came an army of ants,
        commissioned and driven.
And they worked until the task was done.
They did it.

By noon, "I am half way there", I thought.
"Must I stop, walk back to base, or
        must I continue to climb?"
Truthfully, going either way is a test.
But I must decide, which I will take
            and act.

So the climb to the mountain top
        continued.
And often, I pleasantly felt
    the freshness and fragrance of God.
And I knew that He was close,
        as close as the air.
This was an electric moment.

So I kept climbing.
The falling rocks were as music at my feet.
My dripping sweat cooled
        my fatigued frame.
My pounding heart pushed me forward
            like the wind.
So I kept climbing, and climbing
    higher and higher.
The night-fall brought me
    the starry heavens.

The falling rain seasoned the air
 with newness.
The singing night birds taught me
 new songs I never sang before.

Then the wonder of it all came –
 the birth of a new day,
  the sun as a smiling face and
   the morning breeze, like
    music and a dream of two lovers.

So I kept climbing,
 climbing closer to the mountain top.
Suddenly, there was a silence.
The drum of heart beats was
 the only voice that spoke.
For ecstasy had put reality and pain
 to silence.
Yes, there I was
 standing on the mountain top,
  my dream of glory,
   the face of true love
    the dream of lovers.
And sitting there waiting for me
 on the mountain top,
  with my name inscribed, was
   a cut of precious diamond.
It was mine.
 Forever,
  mine.

MUSHROOMS

The Lord knows
    that my favorite desert is carrot cake.
Yes, this is my delight.
Whenever carrot cake comes my way
    my lips always say, yes.

There have been times, it seemed,
    when the Lord Himself, served me
        carrot cake.
And this brought us so much closer.
And He knew that.

One day, someone brought me a package.
No, it was not carrot cake inside.
The package contained mushrooms,
    my strongest dislike.
So I asked the Lord –
    why it came to me,
      and why mushrooms,
        and why I should eat
          this tasteless substance.

The Lord insisted that
    eating was more important
      than questioning
        and that I should eat.

How do I do this?

Well, it took forever
    to fork, to position, to encounter
        this undesirable substance.
And I was amazed the next day
    to realize that I was still living
        and doing well.

Months later,
    the Lord and I were exchanging ideas.
I inquired about the package of
        mushrooms
        and why He allowed it
            to come my way
            and even worse,
                He insisted that I ate them.
Why Lord?

Then the Lord explained it all to me –

There was coming upon the land
    an epidemic.
Many would be plagued with this.
Many would suffer severely.
Many would be seized with
    permanent paralysis.
Many would even die.
And those who would be immune
    to this epidemic,
        would be those who ate this
            mushroom.

Then I realized,
   how much God loves me,
     through a package of mushrooms,
      my strongest dislike,
       and how it saved my life.

Then I realized,
   that some things
     may have no taste,
      but they might have
       life

I am learning
   that even though I may not
   understand the Lord,
     my life is safe
      when directed by Him.

Even when mushrooms
   are His serving to me.

Plant a flower and watch it grow

JOY

The joy
  that walks with me,
   is the joy that walks with God.

The only joy
  that is real joy
   is God's joy,
    which is my delight.

This joy ,
  is God's riches
   imparted to mc.

This joy,
  is free
   to soar in and around me.

If this joy
  lingers away in the clouds,
    no other joy
     can take its place.

In this joy,
  the condition lies
   in the taking
    at my choosing.

While other joys
    fade in time,
        my joy is new
            every morning.

Strong joy
    fears no foe.
It pierces through
    enemies lines.

Sharing joys
    is mine to give
        to the weary.
It receives momentum
    in its travel.

Sleeping joy
    is my rest
        at night.
It warms me to sleep.

Joy,
    is in the Lord,
        in the way of
            Jesus.
I love my joy.
Marvelous joy.
Miraculous joy.

GO TO SLEEP

It was a long flight from Hong Kong
    to Vancouver, Canada.
The lights in the heart of the
   giant 747 aircraft were still.
There was only a soft hum of the
    engines as it peeped through
      the cabin walls.
The seats were all reclined,
     except for one or two,
   with a starry light from above.
Even my dear heart and seat partner
     was as still as the night.
So there, alone, I was left
   to be with myself.

I released the window shade beside me,
     just to see what might be
      happening outside.
O, there they were –
   the spread of white clouds
    like a blanket over the earth.
They were lighted by the smile
   of their companion, the moon.
Yes, the moon stood alone,
   but not too far away, it seemed.
 And I knew that God was
     somewhere close.
 And I was comforted and cuddled.

45

My mind gently wandered
    to the path of reality.
I was 33,000 feet from solid earth,
    at the moving speed of
        650 miles per hour.
And I wondered how the pilots
    were doing at the controls.
    "Could they possibly do
        anything wrong
    and what would happen
    to the 200 plus lives,
        including mine?"

In that moment, Jesus walked over to me.
He seemed surprised that
    I was still awake,
        since everything was quiet.
But He understood my hidden thoughts
        and had a word for me.
So He handed me a pillow, then a smile
    and said: "My son, **Go To Sleep**."

He then turned to leave.
I called for Him. "Jesus"
He then turned and came back to me.
"Jesus, where are you going?" I inquired.
"I am returning to the cockpit" He replied.
"I have been there because of you,
        ever since you left home.
 There was never a step that you took
        and I was not there with you.
I am still with you.

Everything is going to be all right.
So now my son, please
   Go To Sleep"

Seemingly, that was all that I
     needed to hear.
For as His figure became hidden,
  my mind and eyes fell asleep.
I slept, cuddled by His words –
  "My son, **Go To Sleep**."
For in these three words,
 was planted the divine assurance,
   that when Jesus is in charge,
     all is well.

Far beyond that September night
   in the air, I continue
    my journey of life.
And on this journey, are
 wild chilling surprises.
They spray thorns in my paths.
They construct road blocks for me.
They deflate my safety air bags.
Yes, they just make my journey
   a roaring sea.
But I shall continue my journey,
  cuddled by the words of Jesus –
    "My son,
    Go To Sleep."
I shall - **Go To Sleep.**

I will recline my life in God's care.
I will not stay awake and worry,
    when I can change nothing.
He is big enough,
    to see me through,
        while I sleep.
And all will be well.
So here I go –
    I am going to sleep.

**GOD'S LOVE IS TOO BIG
TO MISS IT**

WHAT I WANT TO BE

I want to be, dear Lord,
   That person You promised.
I want to be,
      the cherry of Your dream.

I want to sit, dear Lord
      where it is close and warm,
         that place, where Your heart
               touches mine.

I want to be, dear Lord,
      that person You light.
I want to be,
      that star shinning still
         through the clouds.

I want to be, dear Lord,
      that tree standing straight,
            tall and strong,
      that tree on the mountain top
            smiling at the sun.

I want to be, dear Lord,
    the wind that passes Your heart,
        that brings freshness and cooling
        that shares vigor and hope
            to the weary.

What I want to be, dear Lord,
        most of all,
            is You.
                and only You.

**Everyday, Everywhere,
Somebody, is longing for love.
Where will love come from?**

A Letter To God

Dear God:

Today is Sabbath.
In fact, the sun has just set.
This was a peaceful Sabbath.
It was Easter Sabbath.

It was communion at Church.
Something happencd.
There was a feeling, new and strong.
I never felt like this before.

If I were back in time
  and back in Palestine,
    on this day,
I would find the place where Jesus
  was, asleep and entombed.
And I would be sad, even in tears.

Why would I feel this way?
Because Jesus my Savior was dead.
And we would no longer
  go on walks.
Maybe, never to walk together again.

God, I know You understand.
For something happened inside You,
   when You both said goodbye
      so long ago, as Jesus began
         His journey for earth.

But God, I know that,
   today, my Jesus is alive and well.
He is happy. So are you and
         so am I.
He is where He belongs,
   taking care of business for me.
And that is fine with me.

I must now face the new week,
   with new vision and energy.
You will surely walk with me.
Won't You God?
Yes, You will.
And all will be well for me.

And God,
May my multiple plans make
   room for You and Your plans.

For my greatest joy will be,
   Your presence and plans
      being with me.

So my God,
I face the week with You.
I face the future with You.
And all will be well.

Isn't this nice?

Lord, make Your kingdom
A treasury of Your splendor
A shelter of Your journey
A storehouse of Your grace
To house your dreams
And to reflect Your glory.

Gold – Stars

Gold is hard to find.
It lies deep and deeper
 beyond the eyes.
Common stones are everywhere.
No efforts are needed to find them.
They just scream from everywhere.

Lord, make me to be a Gold.
But available as Stones.

Stars are plentiful and beautiful.
Yet seen only at night.
They hide during the day light,
 at the reign of the sun.

Stars are bright, but not as bright
 as the moon.
But in their quiet beauty,
 they paint a subtle luster,
 to which the night breezes
 whistle.

If you want to see a Star,
    speak to the night.
For the night gives life to the Star
    and causes it to shine.
If you want to see a Star,
  then walk through
    the night scene,
      and your gaze will be filled
        with Stars, beautiful Stars.

Lord, make me pass through
    the night scenes,
      that I may see the Stars.

When someone gives you a gift you have just received a piece of someone's heart.

GOING PLACES

One morning,
I sat, with no place to go.
No, I would not go.
There were too many stinging
        creatures out there.
And, staying home is always safer.

Just then, Jesus came along.
He had come to be with me.
I told Him my sad old song,
        about staying home.
He smiled as He looked at me.
He rested His eyes on my heart,
    then said:

" I came all this distance
    just for you,
    to take you places
    you have never been."

My posture was still and resistant.
Going Places, was not my delight.

But since Jesus made no motion,
    as if He wanted to leave,
        I leaped to my feet.
He helped me.

And in a few moments,
Jesus and I were **Going Places**.

O happy day,
Safe day,
Day of days,
Jesus and I
Going Places.

*The mountain is an obstacle
only to the one
who refuses to climb*

ALWAYS ON TIME

There is no doubt in my mind
  about the Lord's time.
For He knows my ways
  and my needs.
And He cares enough to act.
Maybe, not in my time,
But in His.
And that is fine with me.

Sometimes I become anxious
  about things, big and small.
And then forget that God can
  and will fix them all.
So I look and look, but see nothing.
No one, not even God.
And I wonder even more,
"Is God coming or not?"

Patience and wisdom
  are not always my virtues.
That is why I often move
  in front of God.
Only to learn when it is already late,
  that I would have been better off,
    had I waited on God.
"But God" I cried out,
"Why have You waited so long;

Why have You seemed so careless;
Can't You understand what needs
    to happen to me, now?
I just wished You would
    and I would worry no longer."

Then from the silence,
    came the heart of God, in tears.
And He said, in love:

"My child, I had it all planned.
My plan for you was perfect.
You would have loved it.
It was just like you desired.
And as I was on my way to you,
        someone told me
            you had already fixed it.
And then, I became very sad."

From my broken heart, I asked God,
    to describe His plan.
As He did, I wept.
For His plan, was exactly
    what I wanted.
It was perfect for me.
But now, His plan was
    put on the side,
        because mine was hastily
            put in place.

If only God knew how sorry I was,
I wondered if He would only
    exchange plans,
        His for mine.

"That is not how it works,
    my child.
  Once a plan is placed,
  it is in place. But gladly,
  I will engineer another plan,
    just for you.
  This will be My plan.
    A perfect plan
      just for you.
  I will only request, that you wait
    for this plan.
  It will come right on time."

From a moment of reflection, came this:

It is difficult to learn
    that God is -
      Always On Time.
I am slow to understand
    that God is -
      Always On Time.
But once this has sunken deep
  into my modus operandi
    there comes a bubbling stream
      of peace, assurance
        and victory.

So now, I am learning,
   Not to push the Lord
   Not to speed ahead of the Lord
   But to wait on the Lord,
   in perfect, calm assurance, for
      He is - **Always On Time.**

Thank You Lord.

**When I opened the blinds
Then I saw the sunshine.
It was not as dark, outside,
As I had thought.**

HOME WITHOUT ME

He put together the universe,
    you and me.
Then He wrapped us like
  a gift package,
    placed us in His view,
      for Him to see and enjoy,
        for we are special to Him.

As we grew, we walked away
    from His touch.
And though we are so far gone,
    He sees us still.
You can see Him, as a lonely figure,
    by His window He sits.
And every shadow, steals His heart,
    thinking it is you or me,
      returning home to Him.
Doesn't my Father have things
    to do,
      instead of hanging out,
        waiting for me?

I wish He would quit
    causing me guilt
        and just go on without me.
But "No" He said.
    " I prefer to wait,
        even though the waiting
        is long and lonely."

I am not the only one
    away from home.
So how could my Father miss me?
Well, each one has
    a little piece of Him.
And He is incomplete,
    until all the pieces
        are together again.
So even though the crowd
    keeps coming,
        my Father knows that I am still
            out there, not home.
And without me home,
    He is troubled in heart,
        for He cannot do without me,
            home.

A CHRISTIAN

A Christian is one
who has been
pushed beyond limits,
tested by fire and wind,
been to the dead-end streets
and at times struck down
to the ground,
but who, under all these
adversities, understood the
meaning of the Christian
Calling,
the strength of the Lord
and like a rock, stood firm
and unmovable.

IMITATION

The imitation of Christ
is the song of the humble.
For as Christ served
and lifted the broken hearted,
so the servant gathers
and nurtures the fallen.

Christ saw humanity
from His heavenly platform.
But He walked by their sides
in order to touch their pains
and see the tear drops
on their faces.
He cured pains.
He dried tears.
He lifted tired feet.
And placed smiles on faces,
scarred by agony.
And the world became
a garden again.

The imitation of Christ
is the song that plays
on the Christian's harp.
And the world around
stops, to sing along.

MEMORIES

*I*f you have not remembered,
It is because you have not lived.
For life is a plant, which
   manufactures memories.
And memories manufacture life.

If you have not smiled today,
It is because you have not remembered
   the pleasantries of yesterday.
So just take a moment to remember and
   your gloom will fade away.
For it is memories which open
   the windows to sunshine.

Use your memory as a window.
Use your memory as a shield.
Use your memory as a friend.
And even if others fail you,
May your memory remain forever.

FATHER'S WILL

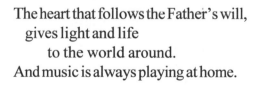

Fear not the Father's will.
He has done it Himself.
He will handle it with you.

His will might be unknown.
But do not resist
 and surrender to ease.
Wait, and wait
It will find you.

His will might be rocky,
 winding and mountainous
But it has no dead ends.
You will never have to turn back.
And remember, you are promised
 a safe landing,
  not a smooth sailing.

The heart that follows the Father's will,
 gives light and life
  to the world around.
And music is always playing at home.

Maybe, the Father's will is hidden
 and seems no where in sight.
Then listen, the Father wants you

to look for Him,
until you find Him.
When you know the Father's will,
then you are a part of the unfolding
of a rose under the smiles
of the rising sun.
And morning beauty is spreading
as long as the day.

Doing the Father's will,
is a moment of peace.
A peace so still, like the particles
of the setting sun.
A peace that calms and colors.

And as a child,
you have grown to know,
that the most essential of all desires
is to know, and to do
the Father's will.
A will, born in heaven,
but migrated to earth.
And while on earth,
earth again can look heavenward.

This is why Father,
Your will is my delight,
my peace
and my way of life.

So please Father,
Walk with me.
Hold me.
Teach me,
until I am completely
  corded into Your will.
  And my will becomes Yours,
    and Yours, mine.
          Forever.

**The difference between a dream
and a stomach ache, is:
One is a real experience;
The other is to be made
a real experience.**

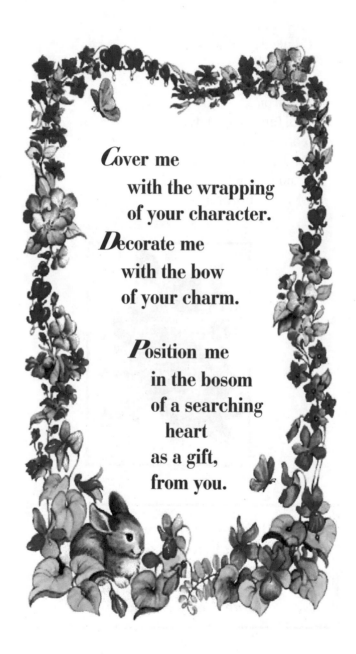

Cover me
    with the wrapping
    of your character.
Decorate me
    with the bow
    of your charm.

Position me
    in the bosom
    of a searching
        heart
    as a gift,
    from you.

REMIND ME

The morning has called
The sun has begun its journey
The mail has been delivered
And I haven't met my Lord, yet
How could I forget?

The telephone has been ringing
     off the wall
The sales person is at the door
The cat wants out
And I haven't met my Lord, yet
How could I forget?

The morning news are as they always are,
     nothing new
The stock market has hit record high
The sports column is as interesting as ever
And I haven't met my Lord, yet
How could I forget?

I am tired, utterly tired, from doing
   all things needed to be done,
    from just thinking of
     all the things to be done
And I haven't met my Lord, yet
How could I forget?

The day is almost over
The night stretches for a place to rest
The ball game will be on, soon
And I haven't met my Lord, yet
How could I forget?

When it is all said
    and the tasks are all done
    I find myself reaching for the comfort
        of my resting place, my bed
And before I remember to meet my Lord,
    my eyes close in slumber
        for the night, until the next day
How could I forget?

So Lord, please remind me that –
    at the beginning of the day,
        to come firstly to You
Remind me Lord, that –
    strength and wisdom flow from You
    and without You, nothing happens.
Remind me Lord, that –
    time spent with You, changes the world
        and me
Remind me Lord, or else
    I am sure to forget.

THE WALK

Around the corner
  deep within my hiding place
    lies my double face mirror
On one side, is my desire to be
    noble and good
On the other side, is the easy path to
    freedom – freedom to be mean
        and indifferent.

And while both sides of me
    are mine to keep
I find a sweet repose in the walk
    that Jesus did.

Yes, I can see Jesus.
He has stopped by the home of that
  difficult, hard to please,
    disagreeable man.
The man is surprised.
But Jesus is not.
For the Son of God is not imprisoned
    by indifference.
O yes, Jesus is offering to the man,
    His hands.
For He knows the power of a touch.
Look, the cold, icy chips of
  that careless heart are now
    falling like a warm stream of tears.

For the presence of Jesus
   adds color and texture
      to the most obnoxious fabrics of life.

Look at Jesus as He is walking in the field.
He sees a broken twig, as it lingers
   to the ground.
But He will not pass.
No, He stops.
Taking a string from His hanging bag
   He ties the broken twig to life.
And the twig now smiles again.
And its parents sing
 "Welcome home"
And write a "thank you" note to Jesus.

As Jesus walks on.
He too is smiling.
He is smiling because
   He has healed a broken dream
      and put a fallen twig
         back together.

I love the walk of Jesus.
It brought Him my way.
He found me sleeping and broken
And He sat and rested close beside me.
For He knew I needed Him and rest.

So upon awaking,
  He smiled at me and called me
      close to Him

And I was instantly at home with Him,
   charmed by His gracious touch
      and His gentle warmth.

Then Jesus kept walking.
I suppose He has you on His mind.
He is looking for you.

Do not pick your neighbor's rose
The next person behind you
May want to enjoy it.

Lord, allow to flow
around me:

A garden of flowers

Water falls

Music

Birds and fishes

Apple trees &
Grape vines

Family & friends

Most of all - You

A BRIGHT OUT-LOOK

When I feel happy
    I will model it
When I feel uncertain
    I will process more
When I feel lonely
    I will pray for friendship
When I feel rich
    I will feed the poor
When I feel successful
    I will be thankful
When I feel discouraged
    I will re-group
When I feel creative
    I will adventure
When I feel fearful
    I will call on hope
When I feel sad
    I will paint pretty pictures
When I feel courageous
    I will explore
When I feel heavenly
    I will look up and around
When I feel tired
    I will rest

VICTORY

*L*et not your today be consumed
   by yesterday,
     when yesterday brought you pain.
And neither enclose yesterday
    in a hiding box and place it
       in the shadow.
For there is never a today
   without a yesterday.
So hold your yesterdays before your eyes.

Look at your yesterdays.
Take notes, evaluate, learn, re-assemble,
  re-direct, praise, say thanks and
    good-byes.
Then walk boldly, triumphantly into today.

Let not your tomorrow be consumed
   by today
    when today comes with pain.
Neither shed tears for tomorrow when
    today is all that is needed.
For though tomorrow and today
    are neighbors
      they are not automatically fused
        by a common line.
No, tomorrow is very different from today –
    as different as ten years.

So walk into tomorrow with
   a newness and freshness- as fresh as
      your first glance of sunrise.
Walk into tomorrow as the day of
   opportunity and possibility.
Embrace it.
Let it not embrace you.
For you are stronger
   than any circumstance.

Walk into tomorrow.
It was created just for you.
And as you walk, remember,
   you walk not alone.
   God walks with you.
   He holds your hands.

So in your victory-
   Say thanks to yesterday.
   Celebrate your today.

   Look expectantly towards tomorrow.

**The window to
   enlightenment
      ...Is Trust**

CAMPING

The lake in its stillness and beauty
   sits at the floor of the valley.

The road winds, narrows and drops at
   times, but gets you there.

The desire from under your left ribs
   and the need from under your hat,
   will cause you to get there.

And at the end of the journey
   when you see the beauty of the lake,
   the softness of the water
   and the laughter of the campers,
   you will be wrapped in-
      **where you are, and
      not how you got there.**

Begin your day with God.
For God begins His day with you.

PICTURES ON THE WALL

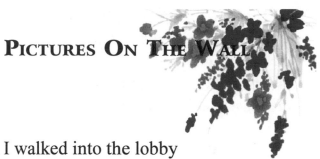

I walked into the lobby
  of the Doctor's office.
There were people, chairs and carpet.
The music of the telephone
  and the occasional fax machine chime,
    broke the silence.
But the moment that bent my mind, was
the contact with the pictures on the wall.

Can you see the pictures on the wall?

They were carefully chosen.
The colors – bright, dull and between.
The messages – majesty and mystery
  of profound magnitude, but placed on
    the wall for us to see and ponder.

Personally, those pictures had me
  walking, swimming, gardening
    as I just idly sat gazing at them.
But from these pictures, came an
  explosion like an impatient geyser-

What if my life were hanging like the picture on the wall?
What would people see?
What thoughts would fly by?
What messages would my life paint?

Then I remembered –

Every life is a picture hanging on a wall
with messages painted for the taking
and having a constant audience.

And I prayed –

"Lord, place Your pictures beside mine.
And make them match."

The one who builds a thought
Builds a dream.
The one who lives that dream
Builds a future.

WHAT THE WORLD NEEDS

IS THE PERSON WHO –

THINKS BIGGER AND BETTER

UNDERSTANDS AND SPEAKS
FROM THE HEART

DISAGREES, BUT STILL SUPPORTS
AND LOVES

SINGS DURING A STORM

BRINGS SURPRISES

PRAYS FOR FRIENDS AND ENEMIES

WRAPS OTHERS WITH LOVE
AND KINDNESS

A DREAM

*L*ife is a dream
  with many mile markers,
    yields, stops, bends and detours.
The length of the journey
    is the size of my dream.
For where my dream ends,
    so does life's journey.

My dream begins with me
    and ends with me.
My dream lives with me
    and propels my direction.
And no one can still my dream,
    except me.

It's all up to me,
    the journey I take,
      it's duration and direction.
It begins with a dream
    and a destination.
And with God in the dream –
    a purpose in the pursuit
    a smile at the end, waiting
      I shall see a dream come true.

I Stayed Up For You

You said you would be late
   for there were things yet to do
      at the office.
And since you were unsure of the time,
   I should eat and settle down
      for the night.
But that was not good enough for me,
      for I wanted to see you.
So I stayed up for you.

Two hours later you called me
      on the phone.
You were not in the office.
No. Instead, you were helping
      a friend in need.
You were sure this would take much time.
And so you advised me to lock the doors
      securely and retire to bed.
But that was not good enough for me,
      for I wanted to see you.
So I waited up for you.

The other night we had a quarrel.
It was over something so simple.
Your feelings were hurt.
And emotions, dashed through the night
      like star fires.

You sped from the scene and left behind
   a broken leaf.
And when I called you on the phone
   an hour later
     you were still uncertain,
        and suggested that I dine at home,
        and curl under my
          softest blankets.
But that was not good enough for me,
So I stayed up for you.

I remember well that Monday night
    you wanted me to watch the game.
You had not done this for sometime, so
    this was fair, according to you.
But I had not seen you for several days
   and had no real heart to heart with you.
And I was hoping this night was the night.
For I knew you missed me.
   "Well dear" you said, "It is getting late
   for you. Soon it will be day-break.
   You may retire and I will see you
   in the morning."
Then you gave me a kiss
    and said, "Good night dear."
But that was not good enough for me,
So I stayed up for you.

I hope that by now you understand
   the width, depth and height
    of my reach for you.

There is no distance beyond my love,
   where I cannot reach.
There is no circumstance beyond
    my embrace.
Wherever you are,
Whatever you are,
However you are feeling,
I will be your faithful arm,
    just for you.
That's why –
   I always stayed up for you.

Give Jesus the peace of your life.
He will make a nation with it.

I Saw A Man

The other day I saw a man
through my own eyes.
The next day I saw the same man
through my neighbor's eyes.
Two days later, I saw the same man
through the eyes of Jesus.
Then I realized
I had not seen the real man
until I saw him
through the eyes of Jesus.

"Dear Jesus,
please help me to see You,
that I may see others
as the beauty of Your creation"

*God's promises are
not only conditional
But eternal*

GOD'S HEART

The Christian has no reason to live
if within the experience of living
there is no real,
enchanting encounter
with that heart,
outside of himself....
God's Heart.

That Heart,
God's Heart,
palpitates with a rhythm and music
that open its gate, wide and deep
opening the entrance for the
troubled, tearful, hurting,
hopeless and happy,
to walk through
and be assimilated into
God's Wonder Life.

Today,
touch God's Heart.

I Want To See You

*F*ather;
I will walk today from here to there,
only because I can see You.
So as I walk along, please emerge from
where You are –
At every intersection,
let me see You.
At every mile marker,
let me see You.
At every railway crossing,
let me see You.
At every bus stop,
Let me see You.
Then my strength to walk
will be renewed.
And I shall make it there
because I am seeing You.

Thanks Father

**GOD'S DOOR HAS NO DOOR-BELL
JUST WALK IN.**

OPEN DOOR

You never know
when God will come
to do His work in you.

It may be today,
or tomorrow,
or even yesterday.

So give God a key
that He may enter
without an appointment
or invitation.

Better still,
leave your door open
for God.

Beginning Of A Miracle

*I*t is pleasant to walk the path
where we have walked before,
because we know the way.

It is a test to be asked
to walk another way,
where we have never been.

But it is the beginning of a miracle,
when we walk the path
where Jesus pointed,
even though
we have never been
that way before.

Spend a quiet moment.
Ponder how much God
loves you.

THE LITTLE THINGS

♥

It was our 26th wedding anniversary. We were in Kaui, HI for its celebration. We were gone for the day. Upon returning to our room, there was a huge colorful basket of fruits and treats, from Carol and Lois. Such efforts to locate us! Thanks Carol and Lois.

♥

This tie-tack belonged to her husband, who had died. Rather than keeping it for ever, she chose to share it with me.
Thanks Fordie.

♥

Lynn knows that carrot cake is my favorite. While at work she went to the cafeteria for supper. She remembered to bring me wrapped in love, a slice of carrot cake. Thanks my Love, Lynn.

♥

One evening while at the Church, Debbie said she had something for me. She had gone to Portland that day. Remembering my delight, she brought for me a delicious slice of carrot cake, with even a fork. Thanks Debbie.

♥

This day, the telephone call was different. For Ruth said she had nothing in particular to talk about. She just wanted to say hello to me.
"Hello Ruth."
And thanks.

This has never happened before. Now it happens every Sabbath morning, with a few exceptions. At about 7:30 a.m., Leroy calls, just to pray with Lynn and me as we face the Sabbath day. This is very special. We do thank you Leroy.

She must have also heard that I enjoy ginger drink. So one Sabbath morning, she stopped in my office with a gift for me. It was a bottle of ginger drink.
Thanks Linda.

On the day of my birthday, I chose to be in the Church office. That Wednesday, Janet informed me that I needed to be in the office at noon. Yes, at the door were the four precious smiling little faces with their mom, grandfather and goodies for my birthday, singing "Happy Birthday". Thanks Barb and family.

A very small sample
of the Little Things people do.
Thanks for all the many other
unmentioned love from
many of you.

GOD

God Loves
God Lives
God Reigns
God Sees
God Speaks
God Listens
God Waits
God Owns
God Claims
God Wins

**Through the Eternal Life of
Jesus Christ our Sovereign Savior.
Amen**